pagina w. 5

D1707969

PUPPET-MAKING

By
CHESTER JAY ALKEMA

Assistant Professor of Art
Grand Valley State College
Allendale, Michigan

**LITTLE
CRAFT BOOK
SERIES**

**STERLING
PUBLISHING CO., INC.** NEW YORK
SAUNDERS OF TORONTO, Ltd., Don Mills, Canada

Oak Tree Press Co., Ltd.
LONDON AND SYDNEY

Little Craft Book Series

Beads Plus Macramé
Big-Knot Macramé
Candle-Making
Coloring Papers
Corrugated Carton Crafting
Creating with Beads
Creating with Burlap
Creating with Flexible Foam
Enamel without Heat
Felt Crafting
Flower Pressing
Macramé
Making Paper Flowers

Masks
Metal and Wire Sculpture
Model Boat Building
Nail Sculpture
Needlepoint Simplified
Off-Loom Weaving
Potato Printing
Puppet-Making
Repoussage
Scissorscraft
Sewing without a Pattern
Tole Painting
Whittling and Wood Carving

Acknowledgments

The author and publisher wish to extend their appreciation and indebtedness to the many people who contributed in various ways to this book. To the children of Wyoming (Michigan) Parkview School whose puppet creations are pictured here; to the art education students of Grand Valley State College for the many ideas and examples they provided, and for their assistance in photographing the art in the book; to the editors and publishers of GRADE TEACHER and DESIGN for the use of the material they originally published; and to Iyla G. Norton of Middleville, Michigan for granting permission to photograph Illus. 15 and 17.

Contents

Before You Begin

Wherever plays have been performed, puppet plays were also. Puppets can take different parts than real actors—puppets can be sillier, more flexible, more elaborately dressed and made up than actors usually are. And the voices representing the puppets are often more natural than the same actors could produce on stage: because the actor does not appear, he is less inhibited in his performance, and he must speak with great feeling to make his character seem real.

Just as in live theatre, puppet theatre requires many talents. Script writers, costume designers and actors are all necessary for a good puppet production, as they are in any performance. But unique in puppetry is the puppet-maker—the craftsman who actually makes and decorates the puppet as he should appear to the audience. This book can teach you the techniques of puppet-making—the imagination is up to you!

You do not need fancy materials to create a family of puppet characters. In most cases, everything you need is probably already in your home. An assortment of paper bags, construction paper, tagboard, newspaper, ice cream sticks and cardboard tubes gives you a good start on basic construction materials. For decoration and costumes, use anything and everything: paper doilies, buttons, ribbon, glitter, paper cups, rick-rack, fabric, cotton, toothpicks, broom straws, foil, construction paper, tissue paper and crepe paper, jewelry, artificial flowers, yarn, scouring pads, fake fur, netting, twigs, gummed paper stars, wood shavings, twine, feathers—anything! And to fasten the parts together, use waterproof glue, brass paper fasteners, paper clips, staples, wheat or flour paste, library paste, and rubber bands.

Create your puppets to fit a prepared script, or write a script to fit the puppets you make. Design a suitable stage for your play also. A table is convenient: hold the puppets above the edge of the table while you crouch below the edge. Put a cloth in front of the table so the audience sees only your puppets, not you. A large corrugated box also makes a good stage. Turn the box so the opening faces the audience. Paint scenery inside the box on the sides and the back, and remove most of the bottom so you can move the puppets inside the box. Add towels or other fabric for curtains, have a few rehearsals, and let the show begin!

Paper Puppets

Paper Bag Puppets

Illus. 1. Since there is nothing to cut, paste or alter, a paper bag puppet is simple to make.

There is a myriad of objects you can use to make a puppet—but the paper bag is the most convenient of all! The flap on the bottom permits the puppet's head to move; all you need to do is draw features on the face. You can decorate this bottom flap in two ways, as shown in Illus. 1: paint the top lip of your character on the flap and the bottom lip on the bag itself, so your puppet moves his lips as his voice is heard. Or, for a flirtatious puppet, paint the eyes on the flap. What could be more seductive than a paper bag puppet winking at you?

After you design the puppet's face, add a body. The slender miss on the left in Illus. 2 has become a whole being with cut-out curves, drawn with soft-tip markers. Her boyfriend on the right has been living the good life—he has a slight paunch, made by stuffing his paper bag body with newspaper. Soft-tip markers make the details of his shirt and tie; use tempera paint or crayon if you prefer.

For a puppet with legs, as shown in Illus. 3 and Illus. 56 in color, fasten two small paper bags to a stuffed paper bag body. Add construction paper

5

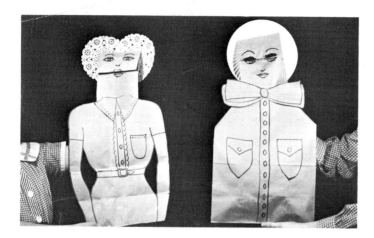

Illus. 2. Paper bodies cut from large paper bags are not necessary, but they add to the realism of your puppet.

feet and hands, and decorate the body and head in any outlandish way you can imagine. The creature in Illus. 3 has painted tagboard ears, yarn hair, and foil eyelashes and nose. Paint, gift wrap, pipe cleaners and buttons accent other features on his body. There is a slit big enough for a hand in the back of the head.

Illus. 3. A puppet as big as a boy? Because it is made of paper, such a large puppet is not difficult to handle.

Paper Bag Fist Puppets

Small paper bags without folds on the bottom are just big enough for your fist to fit into, and they make cute yet simple puppets. Bags this size vary greatly in texture, color and pattern—from brown paper for candy to shiny foil for ice cream. Look for the right kind of bag for the puppets you have in mind.

To give your puppet support, make a tagboard tube big enough for your index finger to fit in, and long enough to extend from below the puppet's neck to the top of his head. Put this tube inside the bag and round the head area with crushed paper. Gather the bag at the neck and tie it with yarn, string or ribbon. The little mouse in

Illus. 5. Perky and pink-eared with a head crammed full of newspaper, this little mouse stands ready to frighten an unsuspecting passer-by.

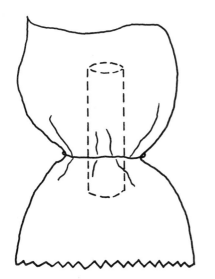

Illus. 4. A tagboard tube inside the paper bag helps the head maintain its shape.

Illus. 5 has construction paper and buttons of felt glued on his body, while yarn makes the features of his face.

To manipulate a paper bag fist puppet, insert your index finger in the tagboard tube, and put your thumb and middle finger through holes in the front of the bag. The paws of this mouse are surprisingly well-manicured!

7

Paper Square Puppets

Illus. 6. Blockheads, made of construction paper squares.

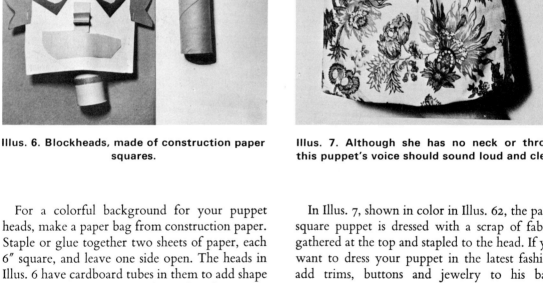

Illus. 7. Although she has no neck or throat, this puppet's voice should sound loud and clear.

For a colorful background for your puppet heads, make a paper bag from construction paper. Staple or glue together two sheets of paper, each 6″ square, and leave one side open. The heads in Illus. 6 have cardboard tubes in them to add shape to the faces. Glue paper patches and trinkets to the heads for features.

In Illus. 7, shown in color in Illus. 62, the paper square puppet is dressed with a scrap of fabric, gathered at the top and stapled to the head. If you want to dress your puppet in the latest fashion, add trims, buttons and jewelry to his basic costume.

Crepe Paper Puppets

Crepe paper is a marvelous material to use for a puppet's body: it is softer than ordinary paper, yet retains a stiffness that cloth, unless heavily starched, does not. Construct a tall cylinder of crepe paper to fit over your arm like a long sleeve, with the grain of the paper running from top to bottom.

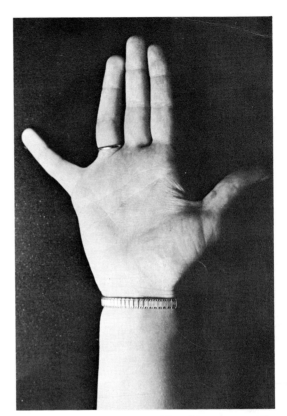

Illus. 9. Hold your fingers like this to move the puppet.

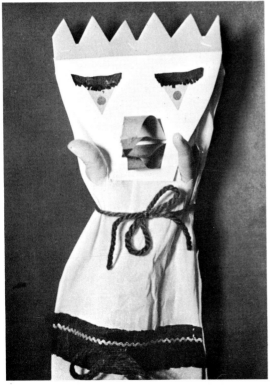

Illus. 8. Crepe paper is pliable, easy to decorate, and comes in any color you might want for a puppet's suit or dress.

Staple or tape the cylinder closed and fasten it to a paper head. Decorate the body with yarn, rickrack or other pieces of crepe paper.

To manipulate your puppet, hold your fingers as shown in Illus. 9. Cut two holes in the front of the crepe paper body for your thumb and little finger to stick through—and your puppet has arms!

9

Folded Paper Puppets

For a three-dimensional paper face, folded construction paper is ideal: it is soft enough to bend, sturdy enough to last, and colorful enough for an interesting background. Cut a piece of construction paper into a 12″ × 3″ rectangle. Fold the paper in half, 3″-sides together, and fold each edge back toward the fold (see Illus. 10). The fold becomes a mouth which you can open and close. The paper in Illus. 10 was stapled along the folds so the fingers had "pockets" to hold on to.

Of course, free-floating mouths are rare in real life. Complete your folded paper puppets by surrounding the mouth with a face: paint or paste a paper tongue on the inside of the mouth—add lips, too! The large eyes in the owl on the left (Illus. 11) make him quite realistic, while the creature on the right—cat? fox? devil?!—has eyebrows of glitter and a fringed V-shaped beard. Use the paper mouth as the base for a bizarre puppet design, like the one in color in Illus. 68.

Illus. 10. Open and close your fingers to make your puppet chatter.

Illus. 11. Whenever your puppet character talks onstage, be sure to move his mouth so the audience knows who is speaking.

Paper Plate Puppets

Illus. 12. The head of a snake with a sly smile sneers at the audience.

One fold turns a paper plate into a face with a gigantic grin. The puppet in Illus. 12 is almost all mouth: a piece of cloth glued to the top of the plate provides a hiding place for your fingers (your thumb goes under the chin), so you can open and close the mouth as the puppet jabbers to the audience. Protruding paper circles for eyes and a red tongue and white fangs turn this puppet into a real character! Add a cloth sleeve for a body; it hides your arm at the same time.

The fellow smiling in Illus. 13 is a frog—as you can see from the warts on his face! Green paint and bulging eyes, made from the bottoms of paper cups with buttons glued on, add to the

Illus. 13

11

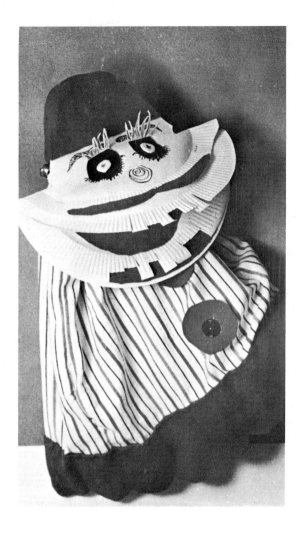

toadlike qualities of this creature. His red felt tongue is especially suited to catching flies.

The moustached clown in Illus. 14 is modestly dressed with some fabric from an old striped blouse. Teeth, cut from the edge of the paper plate, hang over red felt lips. A paper cone, decorated with eyes and topped with a perky cap, completes the head of this creature. See a paper plate puppet in color in Illus. 54.

Illus. 14. A well-dressed character gives an intriguing smile as he bats his long lashes.

Carton Puppets

Illus. 15. Make use of your empty boxes by turning them into enchanting puppets.

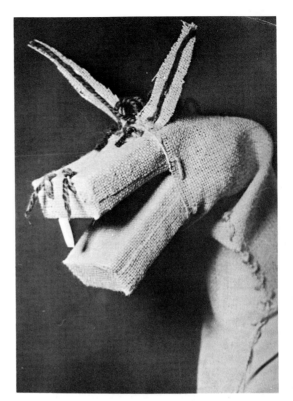

Illus. 16. Animals can be realistically or fancifully portrayed. See this horse in color in Illus. 74.

Small boxes from cereal variety packages make excellent puppet heads. Cut through the middle of the box on three sides, leaving the fourth side as the hinge for the mouth. Your fingers fit perfectly into each half of the box, so you can open and close the puppet's mouth. The two heads in Illus. 15—one a leopard (note the spots!) and one a king with a crown—are covered with patterned adhesive paper. Buttons glued to paper circles form eyes, although the leopard has lost one in battle.

The carton puppet in Illus. 16 is also made of small cereal packages, but two boxes, taped together at the top edges, are used for this head. To make the animal look realistic, burlap ears were stiffened with pipe cleaners and sewn on. Yarn forms the eyes, nose, and mane of the talking horse.

Illus. 17

Stick Puppets

A stick puppet is probably the most simple puppet to make—but if your talents are advanced, you can decorate these as elaborately as you can imagine! The most essential equipment for a stick puppet is, of course, a stick—either an ice cream stick, ruler, branch or thin wooden dowel. Cut shapes from paper and staple or glue them to the stick. Then decorate them—be realistic, unusual, or downright fantastic.

To manipulate the stick puppet, hold the stick at the end. Raise it, lower it, wave it from side to side as the character in your puppet play speaks. If you crouch behind a table or hold the puppets inside a cardboard box, the audience sees only the puppets and not your hands.

Rod Puppets

Similar to a stick puppet, a rod puppet allows more movement and also more realism. A wooden dowel glued to the tagboard body forms the main support, while you manipulate strips of tagboard up and down to move the puppet's arms and legs.

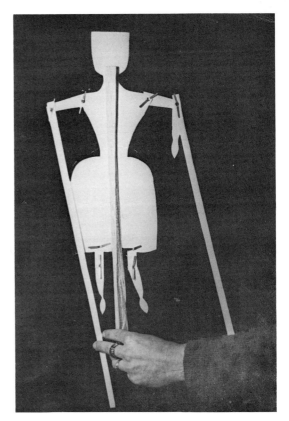

Illus. 19. Rear view of a rod puppet.

Illus. 18. Brass paper fasteners make movable joints, allowing rod puppets to dance around the stage.

Brass paper fasteners at the joints let each limb move independently of any other. The little boy on the back cover is a rod puppet whose right limbs and left limbs are fastened to two rods. You can move your puppet into comic positions with this arrangement.

15

Papier Mâché Puppets

Papier mâché is a wonderful material for the home craftsman to work with. It uses old newspaper (a material always available in tremendous quantities) and flour and water paste. When dry, papier mâché is almost as hard as any wooden object. The puppets in this section have papier mâché heads which were built over various objects. Some basic advice for papier mâché construction applies to any material you cover.

Tear newspaper from top to bottom into strips $\frac{1}{2}''$ wide, or even narrower if you are making delicate features. Soak the paper strips in flour and water paste which you have blended to the consistency of light cream, or use library paste instead. Apply at least four layers of saturated strips in four different directions—horizontal, vertical, and two ways diagonally—and allow the head to dry *completely* before you paint and decorate it. To be sure the head is dry through and through, bake it in a 250° F. oven.

No matter what base you form the papier mâché over, model the head in the shape drawn in Illus. 20. First roll and tape a tagboard tube large enough to surround your index finger. Build the head around this tube, modelling the neck so it expands outward at the bottom, to provide a "shelf" for a piece of clothing.

Over Crushed Newspaper

Inexpensive, lightweight and always available, crushed newspaper is an ideal base for papier mâché. First make a tagboard tube about 4″ long to fit over your index finger. Poke this tube into a ball of crushed newspaper—just one large sheet makes a good-sized ball—and wind string or tape around the ball to keep it tightly packed.

Pour some flour and water paste into a large shallow pan and slide one strip at a time through the paste, making sure the strip is thoroughly saturated. Lay the first layer of strips in one direction across the newspaper base, squeezing the excess moisture and air out of each strip by smoothing it firmly with your fingers from the middle to the ends. While the newspaper is still wet, mould the head with your hands to shape features.

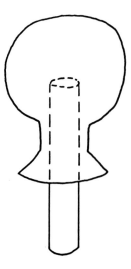

Illus. 20. The finished papier mâché head, shaped over a tagboard tube.

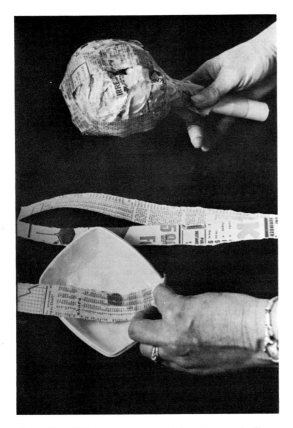

Your finished head probably looks something like the one in Illus. 22. Note the "collar" at the base of the neck, moulded as the newspaper strips were added, which will hold a dress or shirt (see the finished puppet in Illus. 69). For curves and bumps on the face—the eyebrow ridge or lips, perhaps—use saturated tissue paper instead of newspaper. It is thinner and therefore easier to mould.

In decorating your puppet head, paint is probably the first thing you think of. But you can add other features even before the head is dry. Press trinkets into the wet papier mâché—marbles and buttons for eyes, beads for freckles or warts, or a jewel in the forehead. When the head is dry, the ornament is a permanent part of it. Be careful if you plan to bake the head to dry it that the doo-dads you attach can also be baked (plastic beads melt, for example).

Illus. 21. Slide newspaper strips through flour and water paste; then wrap the base with the strips.

You can apply the second layer of strips right away, without waiting for the first to dry. Place these strips at right angles to the first layer, again pressing firmly to get rid of excess water and air bubbles. For a sturdy, rock-hard head, apply the third and fourth layers diagonally across the others.

Illus. 22. The finished head before decoration. See the completed puppet in Illus. 69.

Over a Newspaper Tube

A papier mâché head over a rolled newspaper tube is as easy to make as a head over crushed newspaper. The strips are layered here just as they were before (page 17), but the base is a bit trickier to make.

Roll a folded sheet of newspaper into a tube, narrowing it at one end to fit comfortably around your index finger. Fasten the tube with masking or cellophane tape to hold it together. Roll the wide end of the tube toward the narrow end until the roll is about 4″ from the end, and wrap masking tape around the roll to hold it in place. Apply saturated newspaper strips as you did for the papier mâché head over crushed newspaper.

The little man in Illus. 24 has a head made of papier mâché over a newspaper tube. Pins with large heads make his eyes sparkle, giving him a sign of brightness that his dunce cap contradicts! A ring of foil accents his long and pointy nose. To see a puppet with arms made over a newspaper tube turn to Illus. 39.

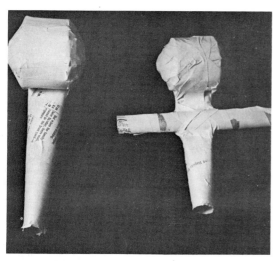

Illus. 23. Two versions of a rolled newspaper tube. The finished puppet built on the base on the right will have arms.

Illus. 24. This dapper fellow has a matching hat and suit.

18

Over Clay

Oil-based modelling clay makes an excellent base for papier mâché—and as an added bonus, it can be used again and again for different puppet heads. Because the clay is so pliable, you can form exact curves and subtle features on the head.

William Tell, shown completed in color in Illus. 67, began life as an ordinary piece of clay (Illus. 25). The puppet-maker pushed and prodded the clay to the perfect shape, and coated it with petroleum jelly to make its removal from the hardened papier mâché easy.

Illus. 26. Coat the clay with petroleum jelly before you apply newspaper strips.

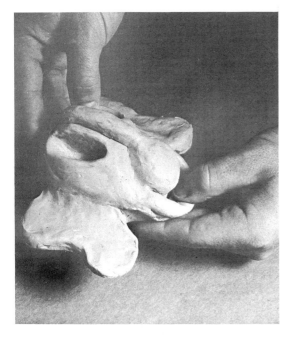

Illus. 25. Exaggerate the features when you build a clay head.

Mould your clay in any shape you want. Insert a tagboard tube, 4″ long and large enough to fit around your index finger, into the clay chin. Apply papier mâché strips to the clay head, being careful to follow the curves exactly. Do not apply strips to the tagboard tube. Instead, remove the tube as soon as you are finished layering the strips. The hardened papier mâché form has a hole in its

19

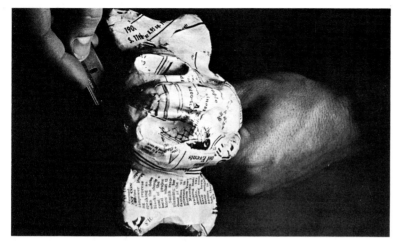

chin, large enough for your finger to enter to support the head.

When the papier mâché shell is dry, use a single-edge razor blade or a knife in a holder to cut it in half. Pull the papier mâché sections off the clay and scrape any remaining clay from the inside of the shell. Attach the two halves back together with a hard-drying glue and insert the tagboard tube back into the hole. Add more papier mâché where the shell and tube meet for a "collar." Use the same clay again as a base for your next puppet head—after such fine results with your first one, you will be eager to make another! Decorate and dress these characters in any way you choose.

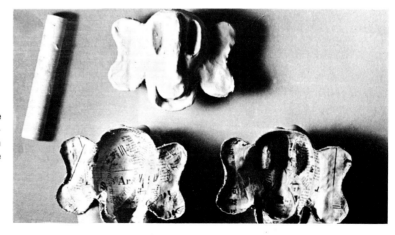

Illus. 28. Cut around the entire head and remove the two sections from the clay. Attach them together again with more newspaper strips.

Over Light Bulbs

A light bulb offers a perfect shape for a head: round at the top and narrow toward the neck. Glue a tagboard tube to the bottom metal section of the bulb for your index finger. Layer saturated newspaper strips over the bulb, first one way, then another. Allow the four layers of strips to cover the tagboard tube as well as the bulb so the tube stays securely fastened. When the layers of papier mâché have dried, the rock-hard covering on the bulb protects the glass inside. There is no danger if the head is dropped and the bulb shatters, as the broken glass remains inside the shell.

Illus. 29. Lightweight and perfectly shaped, a light bulb covered with papier mâché makes an outstanding puppet head. See Illus. 75 for another light bulb puppet in color.

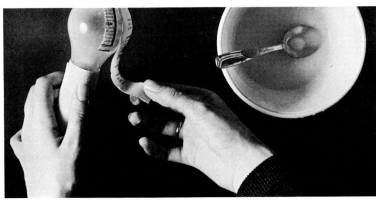

Illus. 30. Follow the curves of the light bulb exactly as you apply the newspaper strips.

Tissue Paper and Paste Puppets

While saturated newspaper strips applied over a base make a sturdy head, it is difficult to shape small areas or make tiny features with. Facial tissue is lighter and more pliable, and you can easily correct mistakes when you work with it by adding a few more thin layers to the head.

The flour and water paste you used with newspaper strips was the consistency of light cream, but when working with tissue, add more flour to the paste until it is like heavy cream. Separate the layers of three or four pieces of tissue and soak them in the paste for a few seconds. Squeeze excess water from them; then surround the top of

Illus. 32. Tissue paper dries to a very smooth surface that readily accepts paint, crayon or soft-tip marker.

Illus. 31. Soak the tissue layers in thick flour and water paste until they are saturated.

a tagboard tube with the saturated paper. The tissue shreds too much to use as strips, but you can knead and pull it into a round shape. To poke small indentations for eyes, use the eraser end of a pencil. Remember to make a "collar" at the neck so you can dress the puppet.

The fair maiden in Illus. 32 has a baby-soft complexion, thanks to the fine facial tissue which forms her skin. From the tip of her elegant coif to the hem of her voile gown, she is an outstanding example of feminine loveliness. To see a completely different sort of fellow, turn to Illus. 48.

Pulp Papier Mâché Puppets

Transforming newspaper into a substance as hard as wood is as easy as one, two, three—just tear, soak and knead. First, tear newspaper into small pieces (about 1 square inch). Then soak the pieces in water for 24 hours. Tear the pieces into even tinier bits and squeeze out as much water as possible. Add flour and water paste (not as thick as you used for tissue paper) to the newspaper. Knead this mixture with your fingers until it is as pliable as clay. Add salt to strengthen the pulp, and then mould the pulp like clay into a suitable shape for your puppet head. Gouge out eyes with your thumbs, pull gargantuan ears on each side, attach a bulbous nose—and, if your puppet character is a talky fellow, leave his mouth permanently open.

Before decorating a pulp papier mâché head, the pulp must be completely dry. This occurs naturally after several days. To speed up the process, place the head in an oven at 140° F. for about 15 hours. The exact amount of time depends upon the size of the head, of course. The modelled head shown in Illus. 33 is quite a colorful character in Illus. 76, and his clothes and felt hands emphasize his eerie qualities.

Illus. 33. Although he looks grotesque because he is not yet painted, this pulp head has become a remarkable puppet in Illus. 76.

Illus. 34. That evil moustache will certainly make the audience question the sincerity of this puppet's smile!

Sawdust and Paste Puppets

Sawdust is available at no charge from a carpenter and is an easy-to-work-with material for a puppet head. Mix half a cup of sawdust, half a cup of plaster of Paris and a quarter of a cup of wheat or flour and water paste with one cup of water. Stir the mixture thoroughly to blend all the ingredients and then model the stuff into

Illus. 36. Although the texture of the dried sawdust is rough and bumpy, this can be an advantage—to imitate fur, for example.

Illus. 35. Model sawdust and paste as you might model clay. See the front cover for this duck in color.

shape as you would model clay. Form the head around a tagboard tube so you can turn the head by moving your index finger.

If you just place a lump of the sawdust mixture on the end of the tube, however, it may crack as it dries. To prevent this, put just a small portion on the tube and let it dry. Add more layers as the first ones dry, and make facial features with the last layers. Modelling the head layer by layer allows the paste to dry from the inside out, making a very durable head.

Cloth Puppets

The puppets you have made so far have one thing in common: their heads were made separately from their bodies. The heads of cloth puppets, however, are attached to the bodies, as the whole puppet is made from one piece of fabric. You do not need to be handy with a needle and thread to make a cloth puppet—you just need a piece of cloth and your imagination!

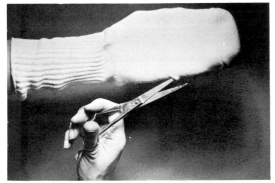

Illus. 37. Insert the point of the scissors into the sock and cut around your fingertips.

Slit Sock Puppets

A cotton sock needs only a few stitches and some decoration to turn it into a wide-mouth fellow like the one in color on page 27, in Illus. 41. Put your hand into the sock and cut a slit around the tips of your fingers (see Illus. 37). The sock has an upper and lower jaw now, but he needs an inside for his mouth! Cut a piece of fabric to fit the opening. Red or pink are the most realistic colors, but that should not stop you from using purple, green or even black. Sew this fabric to the sock with a neat stitch, turning the raw edges of the cloth to the inside. Your thumb controls the lower jaw and your fingers control the rest of the head as you manipulate the puppet.

Decorating a slit sock puppet is an ad lib procedure—anything goes! Yarn, buttons, felt, beads and ribbon become hair, eyes, a nose, freckles, eye glasses, a moustache, or just random ornaments on the plain sock surface. Keep in mind your puppet's personality as you decorate him and he may even talk to you *without* a helping hand!

Illus. 38. Sew a piece of fabric to the slit to form a mouth.

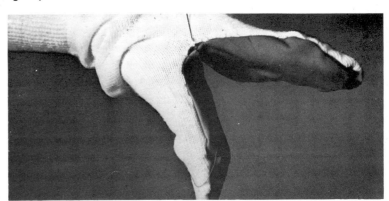

Illus. 39. This chipper little fellow with a bright complexion was built over a rolled newspaper tube.

←

Illus. 40. A silly moppet of cloth has embroidered features and a feather in her cap.

→

26

Illus. 41. Soft and simple to make, a slit sock puppet is easy to manipulate.

Illus. 42. A chorus line?
No, just three hand
puppets with features
painted with make-up
and hair of colorful yarn.

Unslit Sock Puppets

If you do not want to cut your socks, you can still make a creature that looks almost like a slit sock puppet. Cut an oval shape from tagboard and fold it in the middle. A fold in the exact center makes an equal upper and lower jaw, while an off-center fold supports a long upper jaw and a short lower one. Insert the tagboard in the sock, with the ends all the way to the toe. Push the tip of the sock so it touches the crease of the tagboard and glue it there if you want. To work the puppet, put your fingers in the upper part of the jaw and your thumb in the lower part, and let your sock friend jabber away!

The fellow in Illus. 44 is quite a dandy: his elegant coif is made from rug yarn and his button eyes are accented with pearls. Lace eyelashes flutter prettily above his nose, made firm by a rolled piece of cloth inside his head. A silver necklace completes his Lordship's costume.

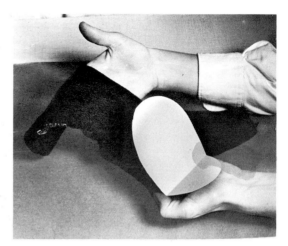

Illus. 43. Just insert a tagboard shape into a sock for a puppet that has as chatty a mouth as a slit sock puppet.

Illus. 44. Long and slinky, a sock puppet can be a snake, worm or any animal with a long neck.

28

Stuffed Sock Puppets

Similar to a paper bag fist puppet (page 7) is a stuffed sock puppet, easily made by stuffing a sock with newspaper or some other material. The Christmas character here (in color on page 31) has a firm head, formed by a plastic foam ball placed in the heel of the sock. The toe of the sock swings around over the head and is stitched there, for a hat. Bells jingle when the puppet moves, which he should do whenever he speaks onstage.

Manipulating a stuffed sock puppet is quite simple, but it depends on what material you use to stuff the head. If newspaper rounds out the puppet's face, a tagboard tube is easy to insert into the crushed ball. Wrap string around the paper to hold it together. If you use a plastic foam ball to form the head, you do not need a tube. Just hollow out a hole in the ball large enough for your index finger.

Illus. 45. Colorful felt and cotton features, eye-glasses of thin wire, button eyes and a black vinyl belt won't let you mistake this character.

Illus. 46. If time is short, a knitted mitten may save the day. Just add a few buttons for a nose and eyes.

Knitted Mitten Puppets

A mitten makes an ideal hand puppet, since a mitten is meant to fit your hand anyway! The imp in Illus. 46 is just a mitten with a few buttons in strategic places and a flap of fringe for hair. The thumb portion of the mitten forms the mouth, but for a bigger mouth, cut a slit as for a slitted sock puppet (page 25).

29

Illus. 47. Dressed in the right clothes, a papier mâché head formed over clay becomes a long-haired hippie.

Illus. 48. While tissue paper and paste usually create baby-soft complexions, even evil vampires like to have soft skins.

Illus. 49. A fellow who needs no introduction!

Cloth Mitten Puppets

If no mitten is handy, or if the weather is cold and you cannot spare one for your puppet show, make a mitten by sewing two pieces of cloth together. Place your hand on a piece of fabric and trace around it with tailor's chalk or a laundry marker. Make the outline larger than your hand so there is a seam allowance and room for your fingers to move. Cut two pieces of cloth the same size, place them right sides together, and stitch them together around the edges. Remember to leave the bottom edge open for your hand.

Turn the right sides out and use the eraser end of a pencil to push small hands and other corners out completely. You can tell that the little creatures in Illus. 50 are animals by looking at their skins (actually fake fur). With their smiling faces and ribbons, they seem more friendly than fierce —perfect house pets! Another cloth puppet appears in color in Illus. 40.

Illus. 50

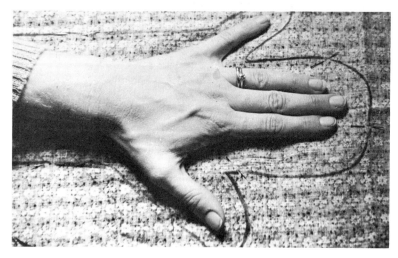

Illus. 51. Use your hand as a pattern for a cloth mitten puppet.

Glove Puppets (upright position)

Both gloves and mittens keep your hands warm, but they make very different puppets. While a mitten puppet might not have differentiated parts —that is, separate arms and head—the cloth you cut for a glove puppet does, and your fingers control the parts. Your thumb and middle finger control the puppet's arms, and your index finger works his head (see Illus. 53). When you cut the pieces for a glove puppet, make the head section wider and taller than the arms.

The bunny in Illus. 52 is a glove puppet cut from a textured dish towel. His head is stuffed with cloth scraps, and pink felt emphasizes his ears. His black button eyes twinkle and his wire whiskers shimmy as he waves at us with a delicate pink paw. See a colorful glove puppet housewife in her best apron in Illus. 63.

Illus. 52. Made from a pink knitted dishcloth, this bunny has wire in his ears to keep them straight.

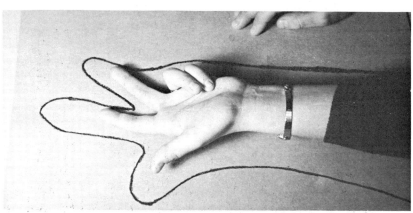

Illus. 53. Let your index finger support the head, and your middle finger and thumb wiggle the arms of your puppet.

33

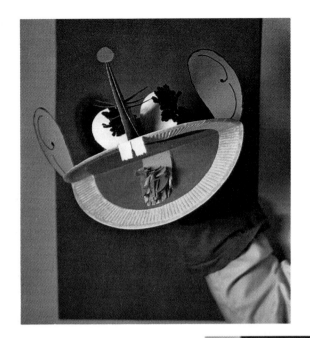

Illus. 54. When a paper plate puppet opens his mouth wide, you can almost see his tonsils!

Illus. 55. While they are not very mobile on stage, tongue depressor puppets have stern personalities that you may require for your play.

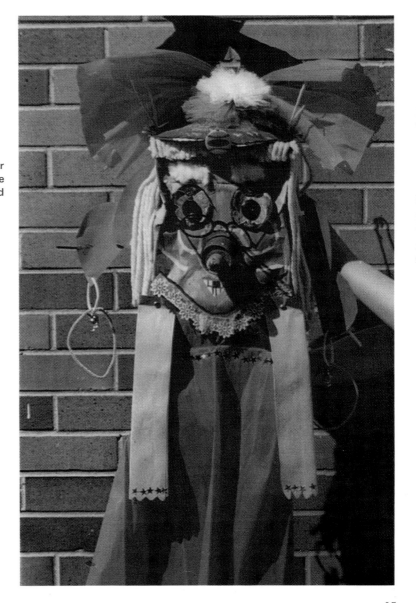

Illus. 56. A large-as-life paper bag puppet, dressed in a crepe paper gown and ornamented with—everything!

Glove Puppets (downward position)

A five-fingered glove is a ready-made base for a puppet. Just slip the glove on your hand, fold your thumb, ring and little fingers toward your palm, and "let your fingers do the walking." The fellow in Illus. 57 began his life as an old red felt glove, and blossomed into the Christmas character shown here. Fluffy cotton for a beard and hair, aluminium foil for facial features and black cord for a belt—all he needs now are his reindeer!

Illus. 57. That old stand-by, fluffy cotton, surrounds the face on this bright red glove.

36

Cloth Monofold Puppets

You can make a cloth puppet with a hard head, with nothing to mix or measure. Cut a strip of tagboard $2\frac{1}{2}'' \times 6''$, and a piece of cloth about $10'' \times 36''$. Bring the short edges of the tagboard together and tape them to make a ring. With the ring in the center of the cloth, bring the short ends of the cloth together over the ring. Wrap a rubber band or string around the cloth at the base of the tagboard ring. Decorate the cloth which covers the tagboard with buttons and other trinkets for features.

The cloth which hangs down from the neck becomes both the body and costume of the puppet. Follow the stitching diagram in Illus. 58b to make a boy puppet and the one in Illus. 58c for a girl puppet. No matter which sex your puppet is, leave the ends of the arms and bottom of the garment unstitched. Insert felt hands and feet into these openings and sew them to the cloth.

Manipulating the puppet is easy, once your hand is inside him. Cut a slit about $4''$ long through the back layer only. Insert a finger in each arm, and in the head. As you curl and bend your fingers, your puppet acts out his part! Turn to Illus. 61 to see a girl cloth monofold puppet in color.

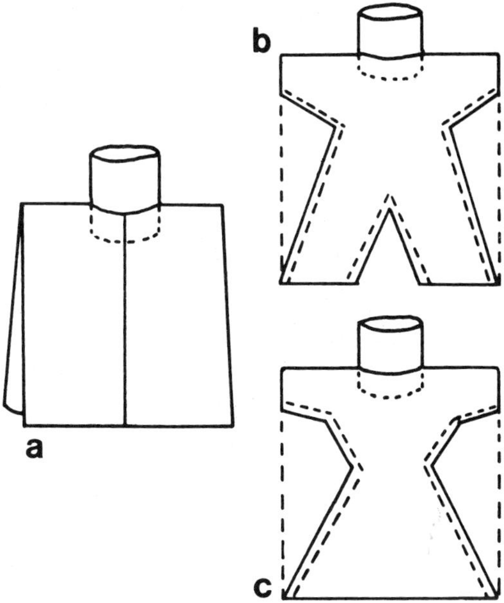

Illus. 58. In a, the unstitched cloth surrounds a tagboard head. In b, the stitching diagram for a boy puppet. In c, the stitching diagram for a girl puppet.

Illus. 59. A floppy clown can be made less floppy by stuffing him with scraps of cloth.

Illus. **61**. A cloth monofold puppet with an Oriental face and costume.   ⟶

⟵   Illus. **60**. A gingham face? While it sounds bizarre, it really looks acceptable.

Illus. **63.** This lass's body is a knitted glove, and her dress a piece of fabric. The head is a nylon stocking stuffed with cloth. ⟶

⟵ Illus. **62.** If the face of your paper square puppet is flat, enliven him with a bright costume.

Using Things Around The House

Food Puppets

Apples, potatoes and other firm fruits and vegetables provide ready-made heads that can be decorated, used in a puppet show—and then eaten! While food puppets cannot be saved for a later performance, they are easy to work with and require no special construction materials other than toothpicks to attach features to the face. Make features from ordinary things you find around the house—paper cups, scouring pads, erasers, corks, rick-rack and fancy paper. Or, use carefully cut pieces of food—raisins, curled carrot strips, radishes, celery greens, dried fruit, marshmallows and hard candy with a hole in the center —for a puppet feast after the show.

The clown in Illus. 64 has a rosy complexion, since his head is an apple. A kitchen fork poked into the bottom provides a handle for his head; you could use a clothespin, spatula or wooden dowel. The crown he sports is a foam rubber sponge, cut in strips and curved into a circle, with metallic stars attached. A copper scouring pad rests on his head like a toupée, while yarn eyebrows hang over cork eyes that were painted for emphasis. His ears are pieces of dried sponge with metallic rick-rack glued in the middle, and a bottle cap makes his nose. The collar is an aluminum pie plate with rick-rack around the edge. The clown has no mouth—instead, you will use yours to eat him later! See a potato puppet in color in Illus. 73.

Illus. 64. Food puppets do not last forever, but when their theatrical talent is not needed anymore, their nutritive aspects are welcome.

Finger Puppets

To represent a large number of puppets on-stage, attach a finger puppet to each finger. The five puppets on one hand might be a choir, band, flock of sheep or a group of "extras"—characters necessary to the performance because of their numbers, but not because of any individual traits. If one of the puppets speaks, move him forward and from side to side slightly so the audience knows which character is talking.

The two puppets in Illus. 65—shown from the back in Illus. 66—are made of construction paper. Since these puppets are small, they cannot support too many ornaments, so the details in their faces are drawn on with ink. To hold a finger puppet, glue a narrow strip of paper to the back of the legs and curl it to form a ring that fits over your fingers. Keep your fingers straight while the characters are onstage.

Illus. 65. Simple to make and attach, small finger puppets require an audience that sits close to the stage.

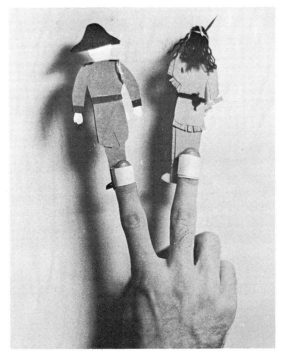

Illus. 66. Rear view of finger puppets.

41

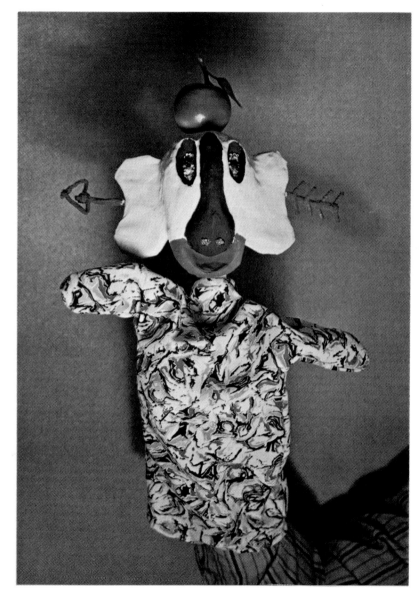

Illus. 67. The famous William Tell, whose son has just demonstrated his archery ability.

Illus. 69. To cover the newsprint on a papier mâché face, use tempera paint. Several coats of even a light color cover sufficiently. ⟶

Illus. 68. When you add folded paper arms and legs, your puppet will shimmy and shake as you move him. ⟵

Painted Hand Puppets

Your hands are the most convenient bases to decorate. Draw features on the back of your hand with lipstick, crayon or make-up. Color the tips of your first two fingers also, so your character is not barefoot. Clothing is never a problem for small folks: paper, attached to your hand with double-sided sticky tape, is always at hand. Cloth is usually just as available and looks a bit more realistic. The center figure in Illus. 70 has a fluted cupcake liner for a full skirt.

Illus. 70. Smiling broadly because they have on new outfits, these girls appear in color in Illus. 42.

Tongue Depressor Puppets

The wide sticks which doctors use when they look inside your mouth are sturdy enough to support all sorts of wild decorations. Tongue depressor puppets are similar to stick puppets (page 14), but this type of stick is wider and so can form the control stick, body and head of the puppet. The chaps in Illus. 71 gain their personalities from paper features and yarn hair and moustaches. They are resting in pieces of clay while other characters onstage perform, but when their cues come they will also move around.

Illus. 71. Set tongue depressor puppets in clay bases and let them be silent judges of the action. See Illus. 55 for a color view.

Spoon Puppets

Tongue depressors are easy to decorate because they are so smooth, but the back of a wooden spoon provides the same surface, and the oval shape of the spoon is perfect for a face. The handle becomes the control stick. The dapper fellow in Illus. 72 sports a black cloth derby and pipe cleaner tie. His handlebar moustache is a piece of fuzzy cloth. The button eyes and pipe cleaner nose and eyebrows are fastened to the wood with glue. Be sure to use a water-soluble glue so you can wash off every bit and use the spoon later—as a spoon, not a head!

As you have discovered, puppets are simple to make. Putting on a puppet performance calls on all your creative efforts, and not the least of these is making the puppets themselves. A cleverly made puppet wins the audience even before the play begins.

Illus. 72. A few drops of glue and some scraps from the sewing basket bring a wooden spoon from the kitchen to the stage.

Illus. 74. A green horse? In puppet-making, anything goes! $\longrightarrow$

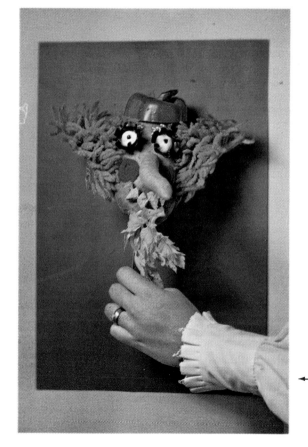

$\longleftarrow$ Illus. 73. A potato is firm and oval—just right for
a head. Add marshmallow eyes, a carrot nose,
green pepper hat and celery green tie for a fellow
who may be eaten midway through the show!

Illus. 76. This creepy creature, made of pulp papier mâché, has bumpy skin and deepset eyes for an eerie appearance. ——————→

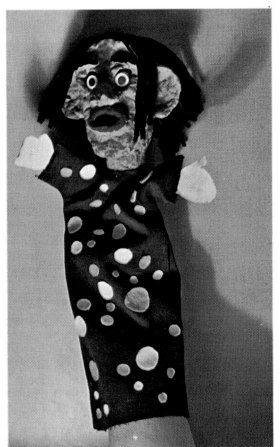

Illus. 75. Papier mâché over a light bulb, paint over papier mâché, yarn hair over paint, and a nightcap over hair.

Index